STRESS
STEVE SHORES

Dr. Tom Varney
Series Editor

NAVPRESS
BRINGING TRUTH TO LIFE
NavPress Publishing Group
P.O. Box 35001, Colorado Springs, Colorado 80935

The Navigators is an international Christian organization. Jesus Christ gave His followers the Great Commission to go and make disciples (Matthew 28:19). The aim of The Navigators is to help fulfill that commission by multiplying laborers for Christ in every nation.

NavPress is the publishing ministry of The Navigators. NavPress publications are tools to help Christians grow. Although publications alone cannot make disciples or change lives, they can help believers learn biblical discipleship, and apply what they learn to their lives and ministries.

Second printing, 1992

Cover illustration: David Watts

The anecdotal illustrations in this book are composites of real situations, and any resemblance to people living or dead is coincidental.

All Scripture in this publication is from the *Holy Bible: New International Version* (NIV). Copyright © 1973, 1978, 1984, International Bible Society. Used by permission of Zondervan Bible Publishers.

Printed in the United States of America

CONTENTS

FOREWORD

ॐ

How many people do you know who would say they
lead a relaxed life? How often have you replied to
another's friendly question, "Fine, thanks! I think
there's just about the right balance of responsibility
and recreation in my life right now. I really feel good"?
Most people I know, including myself, feel either tired
or utterly exhausted. Lifting our bodies from the sofa
in front of the television to join the church group at a
volleyball game seems no more inviting than the den-
tist's postcard reminder to come in for a checkup. It's
not that we don't want to go—we're just too tired.

The obvious fact is that most of us sense a fran-
ticness about our existence, a wearying fast pace that
never slows down. Veteran Christians often look back
on their seventy to eighty years of life with a wistful
longing to turn the clock back and spend more time
with family, more hours in the garden, more attention
on reading and relaxing.

But, except for the occasional physician who moves
to a cattle ranch or the corporate executive who becomes
a children's piano teacher, people generally continue
with their stress-filled lives. Doctor's orders to slow

down are met with a frustrated sigh. "I wish I could," many reply. "But I really don't see how it's possible. My children's soccer league, my church commitments, my cluttered desk, and my job leave me no time to even read a novel. When I'm doing what I have to do, all I want to do is stretch out in front of a TV, eat something sweet, then go to bed."

The pressured schedule of modern living is reason enough for stress. But there's something more. A few moments of honest reflection usually make clear the existence of a driving passion within us that won't let us rest. It feels like fear, but a strange fear—more a foreboding with no clear object than an apprehension of specific disaster. And we're foolish enough to think that if we keep really busy, whatever it is that threatens us with its vague power will be kept at bay.

Day-Timers and regular exercise and the courage to say no to more responsibilities are a part of any adequate effort to reduce stress. But they're not enough. More is required, something that takes into account our terror-filled determination to make life work according to our terms. For reasons that are entirely unworthy, we insist that life make sense. We do our best to wrap our minds around everything we encounter and to figure out a strategy for handling whatever comes up.

We have lost a willingness to live in the presence of mystery, to let our imaginations support hope when the darkness of confusion thwarts our best efforts to live intelligently. Without the capacity to happily lose ourselves in the wonder of what cannot be understood, we feel the pressure to stay on top of things, to manage our lives successfully. We take on the impossible task of organizing life into neat little piles that can be handled. We feel we must make it all work. Otherwise we'll be destroyed by . . . we're not sure.

So we decide what's best for our kids and what's best for our health and what's best for our spiritual growth and what's best for our financial requirements. For a while, we stay on top. Our pocket calendar and to-do list create the illusion that we've managed to tame the wild beast.

Then the chest pains come, irritability replaces patience, insomnia gives us more waking hours than we can stand—and we feel caught in the jaws of the same wild beast we thought was subdued.

What are we to do? Steve Shores, a man burdened with many gifts—including a wonderful wife, three beautiful daughters, both a theological and a counseling degree, a heart that can't stop caring, and a mind that can't stop thinking—has thought through the topic of stress more than most of us. Like all the writers in this series, he offers no easy answers, no "six stages to freedom from stress."

Read his ideas with the hope that beneath the ongoing stress of life, you can learn what it means to deeply rest in the character of a God who frees you from fear. The rest he points us to may not feel like the rest you want. You will have to wait for that until Heaven.

But until then, our frantic lives can slow down enough to let us repair the wonder and excitement and meaningfulness of life. Maybe our weary souls can be caught up in something big enough to keep us going. And, perhaps (but just perhaps) we can enjoy more seasons when life, in the middle of its unpredictability and inevitable sorrow, will seem deeply good.

DR. LARRY CRABB

INTRODUCTION

ест

The good news about stress is that stress can be good news. Much of the time, however, it's very bad news. Lethal. How can we take advantage of what good stress can offer and stop drowning in the quicksand of harmful stress?

This guide is intended to help you answer that question. It can be used in any one of three ways: (1) on your own; (2) with a group after prior preparation at home; or (3) with a group with no prior preparation.

It's amazing how another person's story can spark insights into our own situation. A discussion group shouldn't get larger than twelve people, and four to eight is ideal. If your group is larger than eight, one way to be sure everyone gets plenty of time to talk is to divide into subgroups of four to discuss. This approach can accommodate even a large Sunday school class.

You'll get the most out of the guide if you use both prior preparation and group discussion. Group members can read the text of a session and reflect on the questions during the week. They might keep a journal handy to jot down thoughts, feelings, and questions to bring to the group time. This approach allows time for participants to recall and reflect on incidents in their lives.

However, a group can also approach the sessions "cold" by reading the text aloud or silently and answering the questions together. If busy schedules make homework impractical, feel free to take this approach.

Finally, if you're using this guide on your own, you'll probably want to record your responses in a journal.

The guide is designed to be covered in five sessions of sixty to ninety minutes each. However, you could spend a lot more time on some questions. If you have plenty of time, you might want to travel through the guide at your group's own speed.

Each session contains the following sections:

A warm-up question. You'll be coming to sessions with your mind full of the events of the day. To help you start thinking about the topic at hand, the sessions begin with a warm-up question. It often refers to what you've observed about the stress in your life during the previous week. At other times, it invites participants to let the others get to know them better.

Text. You'll find words of insight into the topic in each session. Sometimes the text appears in one chunk; at other times questions fall between blocks of text. You'll probably want someone (or several people) to read this text aloud while the other group members follow along. Alternatively, you could take a few minutes for each participant to read it silently. If you've all read the text before your group meets, you can skip reading it again.

Discussion questions. These will help you understand what you've read and consider how it relates to your own experience and struggles. Each participant's stories will shed light on what the others are going through.

10

When the text is broken into two or more sections with questions in between, you should discuss the questions before going to the next section of text.

Many questions ask participants to talk about themselves. Everyone should feel free to answer at his or her own level of comfort. People will often feel some discomfort if a group is really dealing honestly with the issues. However, participants should not feel pressured to talk more personally than they wish. As you get to know each other better, you'll be able to talk more freely.

Prayer. Ideas for closing prayer are offered as suggestions. You may already have a format for praying in your group, or you may prefer not to pray as a group. Feel free to ignore or adapt these ideas.

During the week. In this section, you'll find ideas for trying what you've learned and for observing your daily behavior more closely. Feel free to do something else that seems more helpful.

Process notes. The boxed instructions will help the leader keep the group running smoothly. There are also leader's notes at the back of this guide.

Whether you're a group leader or a participant, or using this guide on your own, you'll find it helpful to read the introduction to this series from the Institute of Biblical Counseling: *Who We Are and How We Relate* by Dr. Larry Crabb. It explains the reasoning behind this series' approach to handling problems.

THE GOOD NEWS ABOUT STRESS:
What Stress Is Good For

ε

1. Introduce yourself (if necessary) and, if you can, tell the rest of the group:

   a. In your experience, how has stress been bad for you? Name one way.

   b. Name one way you've benefited from stress.

LEADER: You may have found it hard to come up with any benefits of stress. The following material suggests a huge one. Read it aloud (or silently, if you prefer) while each participant considers what he or she thinks about it.

FIRST THE GOOD NEWS

The good news about stress is that stress can be good news. Why? Because stress pushes us out of our love affair with comfort. Christians are built not for comfort but for maturity. Yet we cling to the "leeks and onions" (see Numbers 11:4-6) of comfortable living unless something disrupts our equilibrium and propels us on the journey of spiritual growth.

EQUILIBRIUM FOR THE SOUL?

Stress will be defined in this study as anything that pushes us away from equilibrium. This equilibrium is a lack of discomfort in any area: physical, emotional, social, or spiritual. All organisms on earth seek equilibrium, and it's tempting to say the human organism should learn from other organisms (from bacteria to chimps) and make equilibrium the goal of life. After all, life itself (physical life, that is) seeks equilibrium on every level.

While it is one thing to agree that vital systems in my body should seek equilibrium (I *do* want my heart to function relatively free from stress), it's another to say the human *soul* ought to demand equilibrium in this world. The simple truth is that our souls are not designed for a fallen world full of sinful people, disease, and natural disasters. Being strangers and aliens here, we long for a paradise that has been offered but not delivered. Our souls, then, are automatically pushed far from the equilibrium that will be ours in Heaven. A fallen world tears at our frame. We are no more meant for this world than a cotton ball is meant for a carwash.

Our choice, then, is *not* about whether to move toward equilibrium. Our choice, rather, is about whether our lack of equilibrium comes through wisdom or foolishness.

HOW GOD USES THE ACHE

"Are you saying," you might ask, "that I can never be free from stress?" I am saying just that. "Are you also saying that I can never find complete comfort in this world?" I am. And not only that, but there will always be an ache inside us in this world. "Do you mean to tell me God doesn't take away the ache I feel inside?" He does not. Not this side of Heaven. Not only does He leave the ache within, He invites us to allow the ache to tell us something (Romans 8:22-23).

"Do you mean to say that the pain I carry inside is *good*?" Not exactly good, not in itself. The ache is there because we are not home with God yet. And He uses the ache to tell us that, if we will listen. He announces not only that we are far from home but also that He has come looking for us.

"But how do you know all this? It sounds like you are basically encouraging me to explore my ache to see what it says. I'm not sure I want to do that."

Your reluctance is understandable. However, Genesis 3:14-19 offers a doorway into the origin of stress and the ache for another home. In these verses, God curses the serpent, the woman, and the man (by cursing the ground on which he works). God is not just lashing out in anger (although His anger is certainly there). Rather, He is, I think, trying to redirect a world that has

15

descended into complete chaos (as shown in the hiding, blaming, and lying of Genesis 3:7-13).

God responds to the chaos in three ways. First, He puts the offspring of the serpent (Satan) and the offspring of the woman (humankind and ultimately Christ) into a desperate conflict. This alone is the source of much of our stress: We are in an unceasing spiritual conflict. Second, He brings pain to the woman in the area in which her design is most vulnerable: her relationships. Sexual intimacy and the use of power in marriage become impossibly complicated. And third, He brings pain to the man where *his* design is most vulnerable: in his attempts to master his world. Agriculture — and by extension, all vocation and all initiatives — becomes impossibly complicated.

In this way, God makes sure we will never reach equilibrium. Why? What a tragedy it would be to achieve comfort so far from home! The pitiful utopia we might achieve here is so far from a new heaven and a new earth! God invites us into stress so that we will explore the ache in our souls rather than seeking to soothe it.

Walker Percy, a wonderful novelist, has one of his characters, a psychiatrist, say, "I seldom give anxious people drugs. If you do, they may feel better for a while, but they'll never find out what the terror is trying to tell them."[1]

ENDURANCE

This is why so many passages in the Bible invite us to enter suffering (a more intense word for stress). Let's look at just one:

> Consider it pure joy, my brothers, whenever you face trials of many kinds, because you know that the testing of your faith develops perseverance.

16

Perseverance must finish its work so that you may be mature and complete, not lacking anything. (James 1:2-4)

Here we see that trials (another intense word for stress) test our faith. Faith, in turn, produces perseverance (endurance), and perseverance moves us toward maturity.

Note the idea of perseverance or endurance. A certain exhaustion comes with prolonged stress. We grow weary under trials. Trials, then, amplify our ache. That deeper ache becomes — if we respond well — a call for faith. In other words, God invites us into stress to take us through exhaustion and into faith. Faith, in turn, staves off exhaustion and leads to endurance.

Stress → exhaustion → faith → endurance

Exhaustion, then, becomes a stage in the development of faith. Exhaustion brings perspective (Psalm 73:21-28), repentance (Psalm 119:67,71,75), and dependence on God (Genesis 32:22-32, Psalm 37:1-8). When we reach our human limits (which is the essence of exhaustion), we conclude that we must find rest in God who alone can touch the ache in our souls.

But we must make sure that our exhaustion is legitimate — that is, it stems from God's wise plan in our lives. Otherwise, as we'll see, exhaustion becomes a downhill spiral into despair. How can we know whether the way we are reaching our limits leads to hope or to despair? We'll wrestle with that question in the next session.

2. a. Do you agree that people in our culture have a "love affair with comfort"? Why do you say that?

17

b. If you agree, what do you think are the sources of that love affair?

3. a. James says stress can be good because it can produce faith and endurance. How valuable are faith and endurance to you, as compared to other things like comfort?

b. How would people who know you well answer that question about you?

4. Perhaps it's a new idea that God's curses were, among other things, His constructive way of putting structure into the chaos of a fallen world. What do you think life would be like today if God had withheld the curses recorded in Genesis 3:14-19?

5. God invites us to explore the ache inside us. Are you aware of an ache inside you? For instance, what ache do you become aware of when you think of your relationships with your spouse, friends, children, parents?

STILLNESS

To close, pair up with someone. (A group of three is fine.) Tell your partner one thing about your life that you have no control over but that you wish were different. Then pray for your partner. Ask God to use that circumstance to produce in your partner endurance and a longing for home with Him. If you aren't used to praying aloud, feel free to pray just one sentence.

DURING THE WEEK

Take some time to think about the aspects of your life that make you ache inside. You may find this hard to do if you're not accustomed to paying attention to painful feelings. The Apostle Paul urges us to rejoice always and focus our thoughts on whatever is lovely. Many people understand him to mean that we should push sad feelings out of our minds whenever they arise. However, facing feelings is not the same as dwelling on them. Even Jesus wasn't ashamed to acknowledge, "My soul is overwhelmed with sorrow to the point of death" (Matthew 26:38).

You might title a sheet of paper "Things in My Life I'm Sad About," then list as many sad facts about your life as you can think of. If doing this makes you feel depressed, resist the temptation either to wallow in depression or to distract yourself. Instead, talk candidly with God about your list. "Here's my list, God. It's quite a load, and I feel exhausted. Please give me the faith and endurance that James talks about."

NOTE
1. Walker Percy, *The Thanatos Syndrome* (New York: Ivy Books, 1988), page 5.

THE BAD NEWS ABOUT STRESS:
Stress and the Pursuit of Approval

২৯

1. How did it feel to think about the ache inside you this week? Did you find it hard to do? Did the ache seem stronger than it used to feel? If you felt pain, what did you do about it?

LEADER: As this material is read aloud, participants should ask themselves whether the sequence it describes sounds like their life.

NOW THE BAD NEWS

The bad news about stress is that we get in the way. God's plan to use stress to bring faith and maturity is not the only source of exhaustion. Fatigue also comes from our own shortsighted efforts at self-preservation. Rather than exploring our ache, we seek to squelch it.

21

Proverbs 14:12 says, "There is a way that seems right to a man, but in the end it leads to death." Two things leap out from this verse. First, the false way is overwhelmingly persuasive. It just *seems* so right! Second, the false way leads to an exhaustion (death) that only leads downward.

What is the false way? We go back to Genesis 3 where we hear the tempter say, "You will not surely die. . . . For God knows that when you eat of it your eyes will be opened, and you will be like God, knowing good and evil" (3:4-5). The basic lie here is simple: God can be replaced! This leads directly to the tempting delusion of self-sufficiency: We replace God with our own ingenuity and resourcefulness.

"Is that so fatal?" you might ask. "Aren't people more or less smart enough to make life work okay?" It's not so simple. If making life work were a matter of intellect, we would *still* struggle morally. But the problem is worse than that. Since we're designed to depend on God (John 6:48), as soon as we step into self-sufficiency we become desperately insecure. Out from under God's protection, we are naked and ashamed, as Genesis 3:7 implies. Since we refuse to take our nakedness to God, we continue to feel shame.

Recently, my wife and I had guests over for the evening. My oldest daughter brought out a school fund-raising project for our friends to consider. My daughter was shy about speaking up, and I found myself prompting her. "Why don't you just read it to them?" I said with a plastic smile that was already stiffening into anguish. I felt a rising heat around my ears. My thoughts were something like this: "My daughter is going to look like a buffoon right in front of our friends (who have, incidentally, uncomfortably articulate children), and I'll be implicated. An inarticulate kid can come only from an inadequate father—right?" I completely lost sight of my daughter's soul in my obsession with fleeing my own vulnerability. This is shame: the fear of being undressed for all the world to see the embarrassing flaws that I really have.

Shame, then, is a desperate need to avoid exposure. We look urgently for "fig leaves" to cover ourselves. The fig leaf that shame drives us to use is called self-validation.

SELF-VALIDATION ALWAYS BRINGS EXHAUSTION

"Okay, I'll buy that," you might say. "I know I'm anxious to prove I'm worth something. I work at it all the time. What's so wrong with that?"

Let's go back to my embarrassment over my daughter's shyness. My insecurity led me to scramble for some fig leaf to cover my "secret" failure as a parent. Maybe I could prompt her without being too obvious. Or maybe I could use humor to take the attention off her. Maybe I could take over, make the presentation myself.

Notice that all these maneuvers have an uncertain outcome. I can't ultimately control the results. What if my prompting becomes too transparent? What if my humor falls flat? What if I take over and hurt my daughter in the process?

Managing shame is impossible! I'll never have enough fig leaves. Or the ones I have will fall off. Or they'll be so obvious that everyone will discover my shame anyway.

All attempts to cover shame are inadequate. But in my foolishness I respond by working even harder at creating fig leaves. It's simply intolerable to think about stopping the whole process. I would rather risk exhaustion than discovery.

THE PAIN OF BEING DISCOVERED

"Why wouldn't you just quit?" you could ask indignantly. "What if you *are* a bad parent? So what?" It's just not that simple. We don't want to be discovered because we feel that we *have* been discovered in times past — and with disastrous results.

When, in the past, we have been exposed, the outcome has often been painful. For example, my daughter's shy presentation of her fund-raising project was a time of deep exposure for her. She had to face four adults with an idea that would cost them money, and she simply wasn't sure what to say.

Suppose I had made the exposure worse. What if, in my shame, I had said to her, "Why don't you just do this some other time?" Hearing the rejection in my voice, she might have said to herself, "When I do something in front of Dad I must do it well or not at all. I guess he assumes that I will fail or fumble. He probably can't count on me to make him look good. So what good am I?" This is what it's like to be exposed and found wanting. The temptation at such a moment is to conclude that one is an awful shortcoming as a human being. This must never be discovered! And so life becomes a frantic effort to appear acceptable and not let others down.

Early messages of shame, then, lead to a life of internal self-condemnation. But you might interrupt impatiently, "Wait a minute! Self-putdowns are *painful*! Why would anyone live that way?" This may not seem obvious at first, but self-condemnation is actually quite an effective anesthetic. It numbs the soul! The pain of self-condemnation numbs a greater pain, that of entering my wounds and seeing that those who shamed me acted in evil ways. How much does my daughter really want to see the evil in how I distanced myself from her, saw her as an embarrassment?

Besides, self-condemnation numbs me in other ways, too. By giving me a way to predict how people will treat me, it helps me shrink my world to a size I can handle. It keeps me in control and enables me to manage the scripts I use in relationships.

Best of all, it keeps hope at arm's length. Hope is dangerous to someone who feels ashamed. What if I accept the hope that I could really be loved, and it turns out to be a joke? It's too risky. I would rather campaign secretly for you to validate me. I would rather manipulate and seduce you into affirming me. That way, I'm still in control. What's more, I can never be completely sure that your affirming of me is real, because, after all, I manipulated you for it. This, too, keeps hope at bay.

Now the stage is set for chronic, self-inflicted stress and fatigue. We'll see how it works in session 3.

2. On your own, fill in this sentence: If people really knew . . . , they would ridicule me. (For instance, "If people really knew what kind of a parent/spouse/ woman/man/worker/Christian I am, they would ridicule me.")

Shame involves avoiding exposure at all costs. With this in mind, read Psalm 32:1-4.

> 1Blessed is he
> whose transgressions are forgiven,
> whose sins are covered.
> 2Blessed is the man
> whose sin the LORD does not count against
> him
> and in whose spirit is no deceit.

³When I kept silent,
  my bones wasted away
  through my groaning all day long.
⁴For day and night
  your hand was heavy upon me;
my strength was sapped
  as in the heat of summer.

3. a. How does David describe the pain he was willing to endure in his attempt to avoid exposure
   (verses 3-4)?

   b. Can you identify with feeling like that when
   you've struggled to avoid exposure? What kinds
   of pain have you been willing to endure to avoid
   exposure?

David feared the exposure of his sin, but oddly enough,
we often fear the exposure of our nonsinful weaknesses
even more.
  Now read Psalm 32:5-7.

⁵Then I acknowledged my sin to you
  and did not cover up my iniquity.
I said, "I will confess
  my transgressions to the LORD" —
and you forgave
  the guilt of my sin.

⁶Therefore let everyone who is godly pray to you
  while you may be found;
surely when the mighty waters rise,
  they will not reach him.

⁷You are my hiding place;
    you will protect me from trouble
    and surround me with songs of deliverance.

4. Notice the relief David felt when he allowed his sin
   to be exposed. Have you ever experienced a similar
   relief from allowing exposure to come? Tell the
   group about it.

5. Take a minute of silence to think on your own. Is
   there any area of your life in which you think you
   should just let exposure come, rather than working
   so hard to prevent it? Write that area down.

6. Look back again at Psalm 32:1-2. Why is it "blessed"
   to have one's sin forgiven? Why is this so much better than feeling deep shame?

STILLNESS

You can close by one or more of you asking God to
give each of you the courage to stop trying to cover up
your inadequacies. Anyone who wishes to may name
a specific area that he or she has been working hard to
cover up.

DURING THE WEEK

Recall my reaction to my daughter's shyness. At one
point I completely lost sight of her soul in my need to

avoid my own vulnerability. I forgot about her well-being in my struggle to manage my own impending shame. This week, take a blank sheet of paper and consider whether you've ever been in my daughter's shoes. When have you experienced someone else forgetting about your well-being because of their own shame? Write down a few sentences about the experience, especially about *how you felt* and *what you decided to do about it.*

Next, think of a time when you've been in my shoes. When have you forgotten about someone else's well-being because you were caught up in avoiding shame yourself? Write a few sentences about that experience.

TWO STRANGE ROOMMATES:
Stress and Self-Condemnation

ॐ

1. Do you ever tell yourself you're an idiot? In what
   kinds of situations do you do that?

LEADER: While the following material is read
aloud, tell participants to see if they can identify
with the inner conversations between me and
myself.

SELF-CONDEMNATION

Our craving to feel valid always chooses self-condemnation as a roommate. Why? Because praise subverts
predictable and controllable relationships. The exag-
gerated imaginary dialogue below pictures the inner
workings of a soul that is both self-condemned and
starved for affirmation.

29

Me to self: I'm the greatest idiot around. I
have lost my car keys for the third time this week.
Nobody could be that stupid. It just proves I'm a
poor excuse for a human being.

Me to you: I can't believe I've done this again!
I bet you don't have this problem. Or maybe
everybody does this once in a while. What do
you think?

You to me: You're just fine. Don't worry about
it. Besides, I like you this way; it's not boring.

Me to self: What if he's wrong? Besides, he
is just being nice because I'm desperate. Plus, he
doesn't *really* know me. It would take a moron to
like me if he really knew me.

Me to you: Do you really like me okay?

You to me: Of course. I think of you as a
friend.

Me to self: Uh-oh. That's dangerous. What
if he really means it? How could a nobody like
me return a friendship? Obviously, he just heard
that whiny note in my voice and is trying to
soothe me.

Me to you: You're too kind. People usually
think I'm a little off the wall.

You to me: You're fine, as I said.

Me to you: You don't think I'm off the wall?

You to me: No!

Me to self: I knew it. He's angry. He was just
hiding his feelings. I blew it again (as always).
I'll have to work harder to get him to like me
again.

Me to you: You're such a good friend.

Notice what scares me. When my friend begins to
offer some form of intimacy, I move away. I use some
form of shame-based reasoning to undermine the offer
and to get myself off the hook for offering any intimacy

in return. This is the goal: to probe for validation while staying away from intimacy.

"I see what's going on in the dialogue," you might say, "but what's the problem with intimacy?" To the shamed person, intimacy is the setting for getting hurt all over again. Although my daughter was shy, she was still offering herself in a risky way to our friends that night. She was emerging from behind the protective wall of distance and was coming forward with her fund-raising project. It was a significant moment for her. If she had gotten hurt, she may have responded by fleeing intimacy and by seeing any return to intimacy as a return to exposure, pain, and shame.

This is why the shamed person obsessively probes for affirmation but keeps the tool of self-condemnation close at hand. That way, the affirmation never gets too believable. It never becomes an invitation into intimacy.

"But doesn't that get old—always beating yourself up inside?" Yes, it means that the craving for affirmation never gets satisfied (because it's always shot down by self-condemnation). So, the shamed person is always probing for new ways to prove that he is okay. This quest for affirmation leads to some serious problems.

For example, saying "no" to requests for help, service, or performance would be practically unthinkable to this person. To say "no" is to close a door on a chance to feel okay. To say "no" is to cut his own air hose. Life becomes a driving blizzard of "yeses" to the most absurd commitments.

Here are some of the voices that cannot be resisted by one who craves affirmation:

■ We've decided to start a Sunday school class for people in the baby-boomer age group, and we think you'd fit right in as our first teacher. We really want to get this thing off to a good start, and you're the person who can do it.

31

- We need you to be on the search committee for our new pastor. As one of the most active members of our church, we thought you'd really be in tune with what we need.

- We're having a church workday on Saturday. We all want to keep the grounds attractive so people won't be turned off to Christ through our church's appearance. We hope you'll be able to come do your part.

- We need a new bass in the choir and when I heard you singing in church today, I knew you were it. We really need a strong voice, because even with you, we'll have only three basses.

- The boss wants a new awareness of employee safety. He wants you to head up a task force on studying our compliance with OSHA regulations. It's not in your job description, I know, but it could really get you in good with you-know-who.

The shame-based person hears all of the above as necessary offers of affirmation for his thirsty soul. At the very least, he will have to do them to avoid *losing* the shreds of affirmation he has gathered in the recent past. "The pastor has invited me to the new men's group, and that's a leadership training program! Hey, I might be getting in with the real power brokers in the church. Just to rub elbows with some of those guys would make me feel a rush of belonging. Maybe I really *do* belong! But only if I don't let them know me. That would be disastrous. They'd laugh me out of the group. At any rate, I'll have to teach the class, be on the committee, attend the workday, and join the choir. All these activities might be enough planks to make a platform big enough to launch me into the inner workings of the church. Then I could really feel good for a while. If only I weren't so inexpressibly weary."

2. What did you identify with in the inner dialogue on page 30?

3. Do you find it hard and/or scary to let people know the real you? Why do you suppose that's so?

4. Why does the person who craves affirmation consistently push it away by condemning himself or herself? What's dangerous about accepting affirmation at face value?

5. Do you find it hard to say no? After reading the above explanation, why do you think it's hard (or easy) for you?

6. After this session, do you think you'll find it any easier to say no when you should or to let people see the real you? Why?

STILLNESS

To close, pair up with someone, and tell each other something you'd like your partner to pray for you. It might be something about craving affirmation or saying no. It might have to do with a current situation. Keep your talking brief, then pray for each other.

DURING THE WEEK

We've seen that self-condemnation helps us probe for approval while avoiding intimacy. Sometime this week, make three columns on a sheet of paper. Title them: "How I Condemn Myself," "How I Probe for Approval from Others," and "How I Avoid Intimacy." List some ideas under each heading. (Look back at the inner dialogue on page 30 for examples of each.)

Next, think through these questions:

■ How does condemning myself wipe out the approval I get from others?

■ How does constantly canceling out my worth add to the weariness I feel inside?

BRINGING THE GOOD AND BAD NEWS TOGETHER

ॐ

1. a. Share with the group one item you wrote under each of the three issues you thought through last week:

   How I Condemn Myself

   How I Probe for Approval from Others

   How I Avoid Intimacy

   b. Then, if you're brave, ask the rest of the group to respond to this question: How do you see these three things contributing to burnout in my life?

BURNOUT OR ENDURANCE

God invites us into stress. He wants us to explore the ache that comes with living in a sinful world. He moves us away from our love affair with comfort and into a quest for maturity. Gradually, faith acts together with exhaustion to move us toward endurance. This is the route to maturity.

On the other hand, we are *not* designed for self-inflicted stress. In our anxious insecurity, we pursue a course that seems utterly persuasive: performing to win affirmation, while pushing intimacy away. That puts us on a spiral toward death. We eventually reach an exhaustion clouded with despair. The text segment in the previous session ended with the words, "If only I weren't so inexpressibly weary." Why does this strategy lead to burnout instead of endurance?

SELF-INFLICTED STRESS ALWAYS LEADS TOWARD BURNOUT

Studies show that stress leads to burnout when the stress requires us to be constantly readjusting to the stressor with little hope of resolution. Look at this diagram:

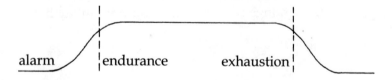

alarm   endurance   exhaustion

The curve shows three stages of responding to stress. First, one's system is aroused to make massive adjustments to the stressor. This is what happens, for example, when the heart speeds up to adjust to the body's demand for oxygen during exercise.

Second, the system adjusts to the continuing demands made by the stressor and keeps readjusting to those demands. As one keeps on exercising, the heart sustains its speedy pace by pulling on reserves of strength within its own muscular structure.

Third, the system uses up all available reserves and can no longer adjust to the stressor. This stage of exhaustion quickly leads to the breakdown of the system. The heart may go into arrhythmias or into arrest in response to prolonged overload.

These same stages apply when we face emotional or spiritual stress. But here is a crucial fork in the road. When stress is part of God's wise plan for helping us mature, faith is the wild card that can help transform exhaustion into further endurance. On the other hand, when stress is caused by our shame-based quest for feeling okay, it more quickly leads to the exhaustion known as burnout. Grasping to make ourselves feel valuable is the opposite of faith. A compulsive quest for affirmation hinders real faith. *Burnout is ultimately rooted in a resistance to trusting God.* Trusting Him becomes the central ingredient in moving from exhaustion/burnout to endurance/maturity.

2. Where would you put yourself on the diagram?

❏ Far to the left; I have very little stress.

❏ I'm under stress, but not more than I can endure.

❏ I've been stressed for a long time, but God is enabling me to endure.

❏ I'm starting to feel exhausted.

❏ I'm feeling very exhausted.

❏ I'm recovering from burnout.

Your description of your position:

3. What signs of exhaustion do you see in your life, if any? (Such signs might include chronic heartburn, tension headaches, pain in the shoulder blades, joylessness, chronic fatigue/low energy, a feeling of being chased by your schedule, anger at interruptions or basic requests like, "Dad, can I play with you?")

4. What stresses would disappear from your life if you didn't have to try to please the people in your world?

5. What stresses would remain even if you were totally trusting God?

LEADER: Read this section aloud, while each person considers how he or she resembles the seals and otters, or the prison camp inmates.

HOPE OF RESOLUTION

Burnout comes when we constantly readjust to a stressor with little hope of resolution. But the "wild card" of faith intervenes to bring the hope of resolution. Faith increasingly enables us to explore the ache within and to conclude that it is simply too deep to be touched by momentary, manipulated affirmations from others. Faith enables us more and more to see that the ache is not ultimately about past disappointments. Rather, it is really about the fact that we are not home with God yet. Our ache is a missing of our "Abba" (Galatians 4:6), our Daddy (who, by the way, is so complete as a Parent that He also has all the qualities of a perfect mother).

We're so tired of living in a world we aren't designed for. Though we were created for a home of security and love, we live in a fouled disaster area. We're like the seals and otters who survived the Exxon-Valdez oil spill: designed for clean water, they muddled through and were covered with putrid slime.

Suppose some of the seals and otters learned to adapt to life in the slime while others headed for the open sea. And further suppose that years later, the open-sea cousins come back to check on their adaptive relatives. Perhaps the adaptive ones are proud that they have learned how to live with an inflamed gut from eating befouled shellfish. But the open-sea cousins are saddened and appalled.

"Why," they ask, "would you want to live like this? Head for the open sea!"

But their cousins reply, "Oh, but the open sea is a dangerous place. Besides, we've had to be pretty sharp to make life work here. And it's not half bad."

The open-sea cousins are aghast: "You'd rather look clever than be free?!"

The adapters are not put off: "Not so fast. Free is

dangerous. Besides, clever has its rewards. How many can say they've survived the oil as we have?"

THE THIRD ALTERNATIVE

We find ourselves cheering for the open-sea bunch. Like them, we long to be free from our fouled and putrid imprisonment in this world. But then we realize something: We *can't* "head for the open sea." That would amount to escaping this world altogether and heading for Heaven. I wish it were that easy! But, for now, we're stuck with this world.

On the other hand, when we acquiesce and adapt to this world, we invite burnout. Adaptation involves pretending that we can call this world home. It involves pretending not to notice the violation of our souls that inundates us every day. So, if we can't escape and shouldn't pretend, what then?

Here is where we need to change the picture from an oil slick to a prison camp. Imagine an Auschwitz — grim, foreboding, hopeless — in which there are two groups of prisoners. One group is the flunkies. These poor souls have adapted to prison life by identifying with their captors and becoming their servants. These informers and stooges squeal on their fellow prisoners in exchange for some miserable amenities: an extra potato here, a blanket there. In their wake, they leave divisiveness, bitterness, and woe. They deepen the misery of the other prisoners in the camp.

The other group consists of the steadfast. Aware of opportunities to betray one another, they instead choose service and sacrifice: giving an extra potato here, going without a blanket there.

Let's think about this second group. Is the prison camp still a prison camp? Yes. There are still gray walls, work details, misery on every hand. But is the camp a different place because of the leavening effect of this

40

group? Perhaps the answer is best expressed in a prayer found by the soldiers who liberated the death camp Ravensbruck. It was found near the body of a dead child and was written on wrapping paper:

> O Lord,
> remember not only the men and women of
>   goodwill
> but also those of ill will.
> But do not remember the suffering they have
>   inflicted on us.
> Remember the fruits we brought to this suffering,
> our comradeship, our loyalty, our humility,
> the courage, the generosity,
> the greatness of heart which has grown out of
>   all this.
> And when they come to judgment,
> let all the fruits that we have borne
> be their forgiveness. Amen.[1]

Can anyone doubt that the presence of such a spirit transformed the death camp? It was still a death camp, but it had a kernel of life within it. This was a person whose spirit refused to identify with the captors, instead choosing to love them. This person's soul chose not to pretend it could adapt to a strange, toxic place. We see a humble refusal to overcome evil with evil.

Much of our stress and fatigue stems from efforts to overcome the evil of a fallen, sinful world with the evil of self-sufficiency. We live in a world we were not designed for. It's useless to seek to adapt to it by a compulsive struggle to be affirmed and feel okay about ourselves. These are attempts to pretend we can replace the concentration camp with a home of our own making. But we are not home, and pretending we can be is the root of much exhaustion.

41

PERSONAL SUFFERING

Everyone has a different experience of living in a fallen world. No two people have the same oil slick, the same prison-camp sufferings. Yet every one of us carries the ache of an imperfect world inside. That ache comes from past events (the loss of a parent or the presence of an abusive one) and present ones (an unresponsive spouse, a dead-end job).

6. Can you think of relationships and events in your life that were or are deeply disappointing? What aspects of your life have suggested an oil slick or a concentration camp?

7. In what ways do you identify with the prisoners who focused on *survival* in the death camp? (What kinds of things do you do to survive? What are your main strategies for compromising with a sinful world to make it livable? Some examples are trying to be perfect, avoiding intimacy, hiding in work, becoming the slave of an abuser, abusing others, and so on.)

8. In what ways do you identify with the prisoners who focused on *making a difference* in the death camp? (What kinds of things do you do to make a difference?)

9. What's hard about following the example of the second group of prisoners?

10. Think about our prison—in which all our survival strategies will ultimately fail. How does this fact affect your view of Heaven?

STILLNESS

Pair off, and tell your partner one reason why you find it hard to stop focusing on survival. Then pray for him or her. For instance, you might ask God to provide courage for your partner to let go of those foolish survival strategies. Or, you could ask Him to increase your partner's longing for Heaven.

DURING THE WEEK

At the top of a clean sheet of paper, write the title "How I Try to Pretend This World Is Home." Then start daydreaming and brainstorming. Set a timer for fifteen minutes, and during that time, just write. Write whatever comes to mind, nonstop, without worrying about spelling or editing. You can write "prison camp" or some other phrase over and over until a fragment of the picture occurs to you. Think about survival efforts in your family relationships, in your work, in your spiritual life. Bring this with you to your next meeting.

NOTE
1. Alan Jones, *Passion for Pilgrimage* (San Francisco, CA: HarperSan Francisco, 1989), page 134.

TURNING FOR HOME

ॡ

1. Tell the group what you learned from writing about "How I Try to Pretend This World Is Home."

LEADER: As the participants listen to the following, they should think about the size of their appetite.

APPETITES

Jesus tells a story about a young man who launches out to live on his own.

> After he had spent everything, there was a severe famine in that whole country, and he began to be in need. So he went and hired himself out to a citizen of that country, who sent him to his fields to feed

pigs. He longed to fill his stomach with the pods that the pigs were eating, but no one gave him anything. (Luke 15:14-16)

Like the ache in this starving man's stomach, our ache is simply not going to be touched by compulsive efforts at "sty-decoration." Getting others to affirm us, to applaud us, to allow us to be overly dependent on them—none of this does more than tinker with the decor. Those who are designed for a new heaven and a new earth will not become whole by bathing a sinful world in rose-colored lights.

THE DANGER OF HOPE

Faith is the willingness to see beyond this world to the great consummation. When we consider the banquet halls we will someday fill with our shouts of praise; when we consider the tables groaning with rich food and lavish adornments; when we consider the stories we will tell of both victory and pain turned into joy—all these coming glories reveal that our current appetites are wrong, not because they are too large, but because they are too small.

Self-condemnation shrinks our world to manageable proportions and deceives us into thinking our appetites are small enough to be satisfied through our own maneuvering. So, for example, we live for the approving smile of a friend. We are so desperate that we are willing to manipulate for it. When we get it, we feel a rush of satisfaction (the same basic initial pleasure a drug addict feels). Almost immediately, though, we begin to tear our satisfaction apart: "If he really knew me, he would be sneering instead of smiling." Self-condemnation moves in and prevents hope from taking root. *Hope is too dangerous.*

Hope is dangerous partly because we are unsure of,

even cynical about, God's character. We may be able to rattle off His attributes, but it's another thing to be sure about His character. We remain unpersuaded that He is trustworthy *in the present.* We may be devoted to our view of the end times and the next life, but it is God's present character more than His future program that injects vitality into faith.

So, what about it? Is God trustworthy *right now?* That question is unanswerable until we answer this one: trustworthy for what? Going to Him for a cooperative world, well-oiled circumstances, and smooth relationships will be an exercise in frustration. If those things were readily available *now,* why would we need Heaven?

THE FOOLISHNESS OF GOD

Right now God is far more interested in providing growing glimpses into His compelling heart. Why is He compelling? Because He loves us so thoroughly that He looks like a fool to the untrained eye. Let's go back to the story of the rebel pig-keeper to explore God's extravagant foolishness in loving us.

The rebel headed for home, "But while he was still a long way off, his father saw him and was filled with compassion for him; he ran to his son, threw his arms around him and kissed him" (Luke 15:20). From the perspective of our more expressive culture, it's hard for us to see how crazed this father looked in the eyes of his own world. In the cultures of the Ancient Near East, older men were expected to be extremely dignified, and they *never, ever* ran. The father's running in this story would be equivalent to the President of the United States doing a break-dance to celebrate a Rose Garden bill-signing.

When Jesus crafted this story, He made a special point of portraying the father as plunging beyond the bounds of decorum in his expression of love for his son.

47

So consumed was he with love that this elderly man acted the fool in the eyes of his culture. He didn't care that he looked foolish, because he cared far more for his son's well-being. He went even further by throwing an enormous feast for the one who had been found, an act for which his older son soundly rebuked him.

The father's reply is arresting: "We had to celebrate and be glad, because this brother of yours was dead and is alive again; he was lost and is found" (15:32).

God is giddy in His delight at causing the dead to return to life and in finding what has been lost. He has gone to extravagant, absurd lengths to reclaim the lost. He has allowed His beloved Son to be killed that we might live.

This is the character of God. We are invited to place our faith (for salvation *and* for everyday life) in One whose heart pulses with passion to restore the broken and the ugly, to find what is lost, and to spread life where only death has held sway.

Faith invites hope. It moves toward the radical idea that God is trustworthy, even in a world where my fragile soul has been sullied and abused. He wants to restore my soul. He longs to find the parts of me of which I am ashamed, the parts I have banished. He longs to find and restore the "me" He made. To do so, He must expose and strip me of false props. Only after He has taken away my homemade supports can He show me that I have been trying to find nourishment in food fit only for pigs.

Then God leads me to hunger and thirst for *real* food: the Water of life, the Bread of life. I begin to see that my appetites have, indeed, been too small. They *must* be kept small if any created thing is going to satisfy them. I begin to see that my real passion has only begun to grow; my truest appetite is only beginning to stretch. It is voracious for God (Psalm 42:1-2).

MY PURSUIT OF BURNOUT

Now I am stunned. Burnout has perched on my shoulder like a large buzzard and has bent down to gnaw on my entrails. Here is what stuns me: I have invited this carrion-bird onto its perch! My small, compulsive appetites have made me a prey for every demanding spirit in my world to have a piece of me. I am consumed, not because my circumstances have gotten out of control, but because I have engineered a lifestyle where I am everyone's lawful prey. Too insecure to believe that God has treasured my soul, I go searching for treasure. I am willing to sell myself in exchange for that treasure. And so, piece by piece, I barter myself in exchange for the fleeting warmth that comes when other people smile and approve and affirm.

This brings me face to face with my own foolishness. In my obsession with affirmation I have harmed others, my own soul, and God's own heart. (What kind of God is this that He is willing to sustain harm from me and still look longingly for my return?) I yearn to come home to Him. I find that the gateway is that of repentance. I am called to turn away from decorating the sty, from eating the pigs' food. I am called to turn to the One who has searched the horizon for my coming. I am called to take my appetites to the One who has a fatted calf for me.

When I come to Him in real brokenness, He prepares a table for me that shames my attempts to nourish myself. In the light of His banquet torches I see that burnout was the result of my frantic scrabbling for pitiful crumbs and fleeting moisture. I look across the table, and there He is smiling at me. There is something stern, though. He rebukes me. "You didn't want enough!" He fairly roars at me. "Fool! Scurrying around like a chicken for corn!" He is incredulous. He relaxes into a huge laugh and throws me something wonderful, a shank of veal as big as my thigh. "Eat!" He roars again. I am deafened by His roar but invited by His smile. The Bread of Life strides off to look to the needs of other guests. I take a lusty bite of the veal. I remember the pig food. Shaking my head, I both weep and laugh as I busy myself with the great task of adjusting my appetite. I can hardly believe I almost died from not being ravenous enough.

2. In session 4 we saw that burnout comes from constantly readjusting to a stressor with little hope of resolution. Faith, though, ignites a hope that brings new energy to endure.

   After reading this section, which of these best describes you?

   ❏ I'm so burned out it's going to take some time for me to grasp that hope.

   ❏ I still feel hopeless, but I don't know why.

   ❏ I'm tired of eating pig scraps, and heading home to God seems worth a try.

   ❏ I'm so excited that God wants me back.

   ❏ My appetite for God is expanding.

   ❏ I've been eating at God's table for a while, and it's wonderful.

   Your description of you:

3. What would you say your appetite has been focused on recently? (Approval from a particular person or people in general? Doing everything perfectly? Being with God in ways you can't earn?)

4. How does *increasing* our appetites and aiming them, by faith, toward God bring hope of resolution?

5. Why do you suppose we would rather keep our appetites and desires small?

6. What have you done to keep your appetite small?

7. How do you want to view and handle stress differently from now on?

STILLNESS

Take time at the end of your session to talk with God. Each of you can thank Him for one thing you have gained from this study. You can also ask Him to continue to increase your appetite for Him.

CONCLUSION

Christians are built not for equilibrium but for maturity. Maturity is developed, in part, in the crucible of stress. Without stress, we settle for a bland, self-interested existence. Stress brings disruption and provocation that, through the catalyst of faith, stimulates us toward spiritual growth. Stress exposes our limits. It reminds us that we are creatures, not the Creator, and that as creatures we are designed to be dependent.

On the other hand, our limitations draw us toward self-sufficiency. Our uncertainties about and distortions of God tempt us toward other sources of security. One such source is a false view of ourselves that emerges from early shame and aims for a comfort zone based on prediction of and control over life. This stance is founded on self-condemnation. When we feel worthless, our compulsive probing for affirmation turns relationships into mutual trade arrangements in which we are free to raid one another's souls. But these arrangements leave us bound. We are not free to say "no." In a life of strategic self-condemnation, calling a halt to meeting others' expectations (by saying "no") is like calling off breathing.

But God is good. He is willing to expose my maneuvering as foolishness. Life will not work well no matter how ingenious I become. Life as we know it is laboring under a curse. It will never be even a mild utopia. God does not offer utopia (until Heaven). He gives a magnificent call for us, in turn, to offer His love to others. The point is not to make the world work but to allow its chaos to drive us to God. Dependence on Him progressively entices us off the treadmill of self-validation and into the freedom of offering treasures from a treasured soul.

HELP FOR LEADERS

ཉ་

This guide is designed to be discussed in a group of from four to twelve people. Because God has designed Christians to function as a body, we learn and grow more when we interact with others than we would on our own. If you are on your own, see if you can recruit a few other people to join you in working through this guide. You can use the guide on your own, but you'll probably long for someone to talk with about it. On the other hand, if you have a group larger than twelve we suggest that you divide into smaller groups of six or so for discussion. With more than twelve people, you begin to move into a large group dynamic, and not everyone has the opportunity to participate.

The following pages are designed to help a discussion leader guide the group in an edifying time centered on God's truth and grace. You may want one appointed person to lead all the sessions, or you may want to rotate leadership.

PREPARATION

Your aim as a leader is to create an environment that encourages people to feel safe enough to be honest with themselves, the group, and God. Group members should sense that no question is too dumb to ask, that the other participants will care about them no matter what they reveal about themselves, and that each person's opinion is as valid as everyone else's. At the same time, they should know that the Bible is your final authority for what is true.

As the group leader, your most important preparation for each session is prayer. You will want to make your prayers personal, of course, but here are some suggestions:

- Pray that group members will be able to attend the discussion consistently. Ask God to enable them to feel safe enough to share vulnerable thoughts and feelings honestly, and to contribute their unique gifts and insights.

- Pray for group members' private times with God. Ask Him to be active in nurturing each person.

- Ask the Holy Spirit for guidance in exercising patience, acceptance, sensitivity, and wisdom. Pray for an atmosphere of genuine love in the group, with each member being honestly open to learning and change.

- Pray that your discussion will lead each of you to obey the Lord more closely and demonstrate His presence to others.

- Pray for insight and wisdom as you lead the group.

After prayer, your most important preparation is to be thoroughly familiar with the material you will discuss. Before each meeting, be sure to read the text and answer all of the questions for yourself. This will prepare you to think ahead of questions group members might raise.

Choose a time and place to meet that is consistent, comfortable, and relatively free from distractions. Refreshments can help people mingle, but don't let this consume your study and discussion time.

LEADING THE GROUP

It should be possible to cover each session in sixty minutes, but you will probably find yourself wishing you had two hours to talk about each group member's situation. As you conduct each session keep the following in mind.

Work toward a safe, relaxed, and open atmosphere. This may not come quickly, so as the leader you must model acceptance, humility, openness to truth and change, and love. Develop a genuine interest in each person's remarks, and expect to learn from them. Show that you care by listening carefully. Be affirming and sincere. Sometimes a hug is the best response—sometimes a warm silence is.

Pay attention to how you ask questions. By your tone of voice, convey your interest in and enthusiasm for the question and your warmth toward the group. The group members will adopt your attitude. Read the questions as though you were asking them of good friends.

If the discussion falters, keep these suggestions in mind:

- Be comfortable with silence. Let the group wrestle to think of answers. Some of the questions require thought or reflection on one's life. Don't be quick to jump in and rescue the group with your answers.

■ On the other hand, you should answer questions yourself occasionally. In particular, you should be the first to answer questions about personal experiences. In this way you will model the depth of vulnerability you hope others will show. Count on this: If you are open, others will be too, and vice versa. Don't answer every question, but don't be a silent observer.

■ Reword a question if you perceive that the group has trouble understanding it as written.

■ If a question evokes little response, feel free to leave it and move on.

■ When discussion is winding down on a question, go on to the next one. It's not necessary to push people to see every angle.

Ask only one question at a time. Often, participants' responses will suggest a follow-up question to you. Be discerning as to when you are following a fruitful train of thought and when you are going on a tangent.

Be aware of time. It's important to honor the commitment to end at a set time.

Encourage constructive controversy. The group members can learn a great deal from struggling with the many sides of an issue. If you aren't threatened when someone disagrees, the whole group will be more open and vulnerable. Intervene when necessary, making sure that people debate ideas and interpretations, not attack each other's feelings or character. If the group gets stuck in an irreconcilable argument, say something like, "We can agree to disagree here," and move on.

Be someone who facilitates, rather than an expert. People feel more prone to contributing with a peer leader than with a "parent" leader. Allow the group members to express their feelings and experiences candidly.

Encourage autonomy with the group members. With a beginning group, you may have to ask all the questions and do all the planning. But within a few meetings you should start delegating various leadership tasks. Help members learn to exercise their gifts. Let them start making decisions and solving problems together. Encourage them to maturity and unity in Christ.

Validate both feelings and objective facts. Underneath the umbrella of Scripture, there is room for both. Often, people's feelings are a road map to a biblical truth. Give them permission for feelings and facts.

Summarize the discussion. Summarizing what has been said will help the group members see where the discussion is going and keep them more focused.

Don't feel compelled to "finish." It would be easy to spend an entire session on one or two questions. As leader, you will be responsible to decide when to cut off one discussion and move to another question, and when to let a discussion go on even though you won't have time for some questions. If there are more questions than you need, you can select those that seem most helpful.

Let the group plan applications. The "During the Week" sections are suggestions. Your group should adapt them to be relevant and life-changing for the members. If people see a genuine need that an application addresses, they are more likely to follow up. Help them see the connection between need and application.

End with refreshments. This gives people an excuse to stay for a few extra minutes and discuss the subject informally. Often the most important conversations occur after the formal session.

DURING THE FIRST SESSION

You or someone else in the group can open the session with a short prayer dedicating your time to God.

It is significant how much more productive and honest a discussion is if the participants know each other. The questions in this session are designed to help participants get acquainted. You can set an example of appropriate disclosure by being the first to answer some questions. Participants will be looking to you to let them know how much honesty is safe in this group. If you reveal your worst secrets in the first session, you may scare some people away. Conversely, if you conceal anything that might make you look bad, participants will get the message that honesty isn't safe.

At some point during the session, go over the following guidelines. They will help make your discussion more fruitful, especially when you're dealing with issues that truly matter to people.

Confidentiality. No one should repeat what someone shares in the group unless that person gives permission. Even then, discretion is imperative. Be trustworthy. Participants should talk about their own feelings and experiences, not those of others.

Attendance. Each session builds on previous ones, and you need continuity with each other. Ask group members to commit to attending all five sessions unless an emergency arises.

Participation. This is a *group* discussion, not a lecture. It is important that each person participates in the group.

Honesty. Appropriate openness is a key to a good group. Be who you really are, not who you think you should be. On the other hand, don't reveal inappropriate details of your life simply for the shock value. The goal is relationship.

Following are some perspectives on a few questions from the sessions, in case your group finds any of them difficult to answer. These are not necessarily the "right" answers, but they should provide food for thought.

SESSION ONE

Question 2. Middle- and upper-middle-class people in industrialized countries today have the highest standard of living in history, if standard of living is defined in material terms. With central heating and air conditioning, indoor plumbing, and well-appointed hospitals, we're shielded from much of the "discomfort" that people in other times and places could not escape. If our head or body hurts, we can take "pain relievers." If we suffer chronic physical pain that refuses to bow to pain killers, then we had best not make our pain too obvious — other people feel uncomfortable if they have to watch helplessly as we hurt. If death bothers us, we can send our elderly to clean, calm places to die out of our sight. If our souls ache with loneliness or frustration, we can numb the pain with television, alcohol, sex, possessions, or any of a thousand other addictive "drugs." We like fast food, remote controls for the television, and easy relationships.

The ethic of the day tells us that each of us is his or her own final authority, and that "looking out for number one" should be our first priority. Advertising reinforces our belief that we deserve the best of everything now. But comfort isn't just a modern obsession. One of the essential features of the sin we're born with seems to be that relieving our own pain — physical or emotional — motivates most of what we do. And why not? Only a masochist likes to hurt.

Oddly enough, many of us will gladly endure certain kinds of pain in order to maintain comfort in other, crucial areas. We'll endure bad treatment rather than risk uncomfortable conflict. We'll work ourselves to exhaustion in order to avoid the agony of shame.

Question 4. There are many possibilities, and many of them look very attractive. With hospitable weather and peaceful relationships, we might be living comfortably in a tropical paradise without hunger or marital tension. How many of us would be zealously pursuing God if our lives were basically comfortable? How many of us regularly seek God out of sheer delight in His presence, rather than out of a desperate attempt to escape drowning in the hurricane of life?

Even without the curses, though, it's hard to imagine that groups of self-centered, fallen humans could avoid entangling themselves in painful relationships.

Question 5. Most of us are aware that people in our lives don't love and value us as much as we'd like. Some of us are intensely aware of the gap between the love we long for and the abandonment we face. Others of us can shrug off the gap because after years of numbing and ignoring the pain, we genuinely don't notice it anymore. We know instinctively that if we were to allow ourselves to feel the full weight of our disappointment, it would overwhelm us. We have an automatic circuit breaker inside us that switches off when the pain potential approaches critical levels. It will take courage to override that automatic suppression of pain.

SESSION THREE

Question 4. The key here is at the top of page 31: "To the shamed person, intimacy is the setting for getting hurt all over again." If intimacy equals exposure, pain, and shame, and if receiving affirmation might lead to intimacy, then affirmation must be avoided at all costs. The ultimate horror would be to believe someone's affirmation and offer genuine intimacy to that person and have it rejected. It feels far safer to push the affirmation away.

The superhuman task, then, is to courageously risk receiving and giving affirmation/intimacy *even though* we might get hurt. This courage comes only when we're convinced that God will enable us to survive despite the hurt and that loving God and others is more important than avoiding pain. Only a growing intimacy with God can fuel such courage.

SESSION FOUR

Question 2. The answers given are not the only possibilities, but are intended to stimulate thought. Indeed, some of us feel as though we bounce back and forth between two or more places on the scale.

Questions 7-8. Some group members may realize that their entire energy has been focused on survival, so they've had nothing left over for making a genuine difference in others' lives. Other participants may appear at first glance to have been pouring themselves out for others, but a second glance reveals more self-centered motives. As we saw in session 3, the motive of a compulsive "servant" may actually be to acquire affirmation while avoiding intimacy. The person who consistently offers her hands to work but never her heart to embrace is not really making the difference that matters.

There's no point in condemning ourselves for being focused on survival. As we've seen, self-condemnation is a clever tactic to avoid having to give ourselves to anyone.

Have the others in your group made a difference in your life in any ways? If so, tell them.

Question 2. Again, some participants may see themselves shifting back and forth from one status to another. Others may describe themselves differently from any of the answers offered.

Question 5. Proverbs 13:12 says, "Hope deferred makes the heart sick." The bigger the hope (or appetite), the deeper the heartsickness when we're disappointed. If our small appetites have been so often disappointed, it seems crazy to enlarge our hopes and set ourselves up for crushing disappointment.

Question 6. We can keep our appetites small when we tell ourselves that our life depends on things like:

- Emotional or sexual involvement with a particular person (or many people)

- Money

- Power

- Job advancement

One way to get at this question is to ask participants to fill in the blank in this sentence: "For me, life depends on _____."